'When times are hard, I turn to poetry: for truth, nourishment and daring ideas that keep me on my toes. It's all here in Afshan D'souza-Lodhi's sparkling debut collection. Rich, delicious poems where mothers and daughters find themselves separated as well as connected by language, where love dances teasingly in and out of reach, and where Snow White gets razor burn. Poetry that is powerful and sharp but never bitter, encouraging us to remember that: even anonymous words / can change the world.'
Rosie Garland

'In [re:desire], Afshan D'souza-Lodhi soars, swoops and dazzles. In this elegantly wrought collection, she upends expectations, shatters stereotypes and breaks a few taboos, but always with a wry smile.'
Adam Lowe

'Whether meditations on her mother(s) tongue or tongue-in-cheek poems on relationships, Afshan D'souza-Lodhi knows how to play with words to move, amuse, surprise and shock the reader. South Asian traditions are simultaneously celebrated and questioned as they collide with Britishness, love is smoked and evoked in all its earthy, unsexy wet patches. But these poems also pull no punches, tackling topics from abuse and racism to sexuality and parent-child relationships. This is a poet to watch - and to listen to.'
Sharmilla Beezmohun

'Afshan's poetry quickly evokes a spontaneous overflow of powerful feelings; like anger, anguish, joy and humour. Her pieces take you on a spiritual journey and makes you question the very nature of life itself'
Mike Omoniyi

GW00471907

Afshan D'souza-Lodhi is an award-winning writer of plays and poetry. She has been commissioned to write and direct a short film for Channel 4 and a radio play for BBC Sounds (Chop Chop). Afshan has edited many anthologies and has an essay featured in Picador's collection by Muslim women called *Its Not About The Burqa*. She has completed residencies at Royal Exchange Theatre, Manchester Literature Festival and has worked with Eclipse Theatre, Tamasha Theatre Company and Paul Burston's Polari.

As well as her own writing, Afshan is keen to develop other younger and emerging artists and sits on the boards of Manchester Literature Festival and Pie Radio. Afshan also sits on the steering committee for Northern Police Monitoring Project, an independent campaigning and advocacy organisation that challenges police harassment and violence.

[re:desire]

I hope you enjoy the poems in this collection

Afshan ~~D'souza-Lodhi~~

Burning Eye

Copyright © 2020 Afshan D'souza-Lodhi

Book cover designed by Anthony Namba.

The author asserts the moral right under the Copyright, Designs and Patents Act 1988 to be identified as the author of this work.

This edition published by Burning Eye Books 2020

www.burningeye.co.uk
@burningeyebooks

Burning Eye Books

15 West Hill, Portishead, BS20 6LG

ISBN 978-1-911570-85-1

in the name of
my mother, the most kind, sometimes merciful but almost
always gracious.

our mothers taught us to love / taught us to love
unconditionally / when a man / breaks glass tables / while
showing you his nostrils / you pick up the glass / cover your
palms in bandages later / make sure you don't shake when
you bring him tea.

contents

iv. does each line have two sides?

v. izzat/sharam

vi. thirty-six times she fell

vii. pleas(ur)e

viii. for my mother

glossary

a prefatory note

Urdu does not have any distinct letter cases, but does have punctuation. These poems choose not to fit into the structures of the way poetry *should* look.

In Hindi and Urdu literary tradition, names usually have a significant meaning. If a particular name's meaning is not desired in the poem, the name is not used; the poet uses *he/she* in its place. This also adds to the fluidity of the poems and flash fiction pieces in [re:*desire*]; in the same way that uppercase can distract and occupy a particular space (namely a formal one) so can names of people.

Urdu poetry is often recited, not read, and poets begin performances and recitations with: *arz kiya hai; it has been said.* That is the tradition that inspires much of this poetry.

i. fresh (i.e.) Brit-ish

what is your good name

fresh men and women who wear bangles that burn
their wrists never ask
to spell out my name phonetically –
to everyone else,
  I lie
        – Afghanistan disused loaded.

her name

when you drop sticks into a pond
the frogs swim away from their spawn
faster than the trees fall
        from allowing
        that last bird to
        call its lover.
Kanta came from a place near a pond,
was using twigs to prod the other children
when the falling branch of cypress
        narrowly missed her head.
she was alive,
no less alive than she had been
when she left home that morning;
alive nonetheless.
but no.
Kanta would never
disturb the countryside again.
that is, until she was older.

she stood underneath
the cousin of the tree
that once tried to kill her
as she coyly called her lover.
he wouldn't come.
and in a fit of rage
        more trees fell.
not of their own accord or
because of birds and their lovers,
but because her own lover
left her unsatisfied.
the trees soon learnt
that Kanta was trouble.
when she walked through
the woods
        they cowered in her footsteps.
frogs found other ponds and
the fields,

they became bare.
all that was left
was a single rose
growing so close to a wall
one would think it was trying to prove something.

Kanta tried to pick
the white rose
but in doing so
pricked her finger.
and so
        kanta was given her name.

burning dupattas

he said he liked it rough
so the next day you
bought handcuffs.

she did the same but
lost them before she could use them.
she'd been taught

pigs are haram.
it doesn't stop her from
sleeping with them.

or is that dogs?
she asked him to show her
how to use dupattas

instead of cuffs. cuffs
cut into his skin; dupattas
cut into her honour.

she lied her way
through his pants, on
his shirt – but kept his

shoes on.
he wasn't dead from
the waist down nor neck

up, so took pictures of *her*
in empty bathtubs fully clothed,
naked minds, long exposure

stopped her from
being able to reveal her
skin to him.

you left the ashen remains
of the dupatta clinging
to his hands when you left.

she is not an arsonist

every day she burns
her own skin
to walk out of the door –
face the world.

their mothers thought the embers
in her eyes were the sun
reflected. they soon saw
their own sons reflected.

they burned her, not
in food with spices
or being love-
sick over dead husbands.

they burned her like factories
making ugly jumpers burn
                    by accident,
by making young boys throw

lit alcohol bottles
into her, by speaking
their own truths for her,
by disposing cigarettes

on her
                    by mistake.
they burnt her by mistake,
told her her plain features

were now cured
by ugliness, used rebirth to justify
their fire.
her skin grew back thicker

with a character of its own.
she grew scars over

scars in the way that amateur
DIYers paste wallpaper

over wallpaper.
but the keloid became her armour.
now, all fair and lovely,
she burns her skin

before she leaves the house.
it is the only way
she knows how to face
the world.

she is not an arsonist.
she cannot be an arsonist.
the only thing she burns out
is herself.

white weddings, white funerals

when Deepika strolled in
she intended to do nothing more
than tell her this was over. loving
married people was something
her mother had warned her against
and somehow she still managed to
do it anyway.

she was ready to scrape
the henna from her hands.
standing over the sink,
washing and washing,
certain this wasn't going
to be a slow rendition of Shakespeare.

she used a pen, only
because it was the closest thing. maybe
it was a nod to the one-too-many times
she'd heard *that* pen and sword quote.
she was bored now.

weddings are:
      long, blood-covered winding sheets,
        relatives whose names you can't remember,
      funerals.
white to mark
innocence and white to
mark death. whiteness forced
into and onto brown faces.
then crying as the body is taken
away.

she had married him
      first, pretending.

blink

he took time to blink
as if he had
seen enough of the world
to not miss anything interesting.

long heavy movements of the lids
catching small micro-second-
          long naps in
between the openings of his eyes.

he never gave to the buskers
but every time he walked past
          he'd smile.
uncontrollably.

he was old. his body starting
to look like words do
when you look at them for
too long. strange.

unlike his father,
who he thought was kept in the oven
much longer than needed,
          he was just right.

but now, his eyes were wrinkled.
seasoned with salt and pepper,
but his opinions became
somewhat bland.

he'd married, naïve;
his wife counted birds
before baking a pie and
blinking away her emotions.

she left him.
one day she just stared at his body
          too long.

appetiser

for the record, Hallmark got love wrong. it's not a parade of milkshakes and *you are my sunshines*. it's pink sequinned bondage ties round your throat, melted kulfi and describing bowel movements to each other at three in the morning.

anonymous was a woman

anonymous was a woman who
wrote romance only in stories
for living them and watching
love die was too hard.

she never knew what it was like to
turn heads, to be the object of
someone's desires, and that's why
she wrote love stories on her body.

hoping that lovers would fall in
love with them and in turn her.
she doubted herself, but her
stories, her words that spoke of

true love, she trusted them
more than she trusted
her own skin.
no one wants to be walking

propaganda for censorship.
maybe that's why she did it.
anonymous, a woman, she
kept it that way. waiting

for the ink to dry, she
shed her clothing.
the words on her skin, a

sign of survival marred with
possibilities and excitement,
Mashallah, they speak
                    volumes.

her father had told her
that the female voice is awrah.
but even anonymous words
can change the world.

the Moghul: Mowgli

clocking each other
from opposite ends of the theatre,
not watching a film, but a reinterpretation
of a play about a white middle-class man
playing a white working-class man.
        Beckett.
no marshmallows for this show, but
cups of spiced tea tea lattes
warming our hands.
we watch sunsets rise
from beyond
the hoe-
        rizon,
you smoking
something wrapped
in brown liquorice paper –
        not 'erb,
you reassure me.
we exchange Twitter handles,
where we describe ourselves as desi activists,
use #BLM to improve our twitter ratio,
yet neither of us have heard of Ambedkar.
tell me that if only I do one thing,
read more racial discourse theory,
then, only,
        it will all be tick tock
tick tock
        tick
tock

one of five

mosquitos and flies smell / maroon in our blood / better than
fresh / fish caught in the sea / but his love for her was / measured
in how many stones / she could throw / mirrors weren't broken
but / men circled around squares / to show their devotion.

2.5 per cent / of a moon / is still / the moon.

3/5 of a miracle is enough / for her / to starve herself / show
she was serious / about him / and Him / and hymns would be
sung / when her hymen broke / during those 28 days / no one /
questioned her motive / they / questioned the miracles.

four till five / became a ritual / she prays 785 times / one heavy
step away / from heaven / she says *hey* and he / responds with
/ *asalamulaykum wa rahmatullahi wa barakatahu* / kneels once
and with / only one look / fulfils her destiny for hell.

five out of five times / I say He / is the only one / s.a.w. the
messenger / also sins /

exotic

when you're only taught about love under palm trees in
monsoons is it any wonder we search for lovers using mangoes
as a marker?

I now dream in paisley

the truth is
that I waited outside your house
and watched
the
          birds
perch
upon
crossed
wires.

they were yet
to electrocute themselves.

each night I hung up the moon,
stayed until it signed out.

even so, between Paki shop
robberies and BMX
bikers, our love
          got bored.

1.5

1.1 last night I cried / my dad came home / and told me an uncle had shouted at him for letting his daughter wear dresses / I cried / not because of the inherent sexism / the male gaze that will never let up in our community / but because when I imagined having a conversation / with this uncle, in Urdu / I couldn't / I got halfway through telling him / what respect really meant / when I forgot the word for *gaze* / I couldn't come up with the equivalent / in Hindi or Urdu / and my mother tongue bit itself / I am able to engage and interrogate certain ideas / in *English* but basic words / and emotions are still stuck / in my mother tongue / I cried because / even in my fantasies / I couldn't win / an argument against my / sexist uncles.

1.2 it has been too long since / I stood side by side with my mother / in the kitchen to cook / scribbling down / recipes for dishes / to remember them / for when I'm older / she switches them up when she tells them to me / adds extra tomatoes and yoghurt and / halves the spices / she knows something I don't / the more / years I spend / apart from her / the less spice my tongue will be able to hold / as desi words / no longer fill my mouth / so will desi tastes vanish / from my palate / I plate my food now with extra spices / an attempt to get used to the / feeling of mirch and pain / on my tongue / a feeling that will grow / to become more familiar as I move closer and closer to –

1.3 my body is one with the beats / of the tabla / but my ears / can no longer / take the high-pitched tones / of the singers / the sur stops / at me / sa / re ga ma / pa / dha ne sa / came before / do re me / but I only know the raags that feature / in the top ten / I've listened to remixes of remixes / until all I can I hear / are the dj / dj / dj / dj / dj wale babu mera gana chala do / but still rejoice when Nusrat Fateh Ali Khan's jaaniaaa / sends shivers down my spine / I start the song again / my lips opening as if Nusrat's voice is my own / but still / even with his voice / guiding mine / I miss / the beat and start / the next line too early / my body / moves a half-beat off the tabla / I pretend I'm listening in / double time / double time.

1.4 women do not fit into saris / saris are made for whole
women / 1.0 women / for those of us that are 1.4 women /
the yards don't stretch enough / to make the right number
of pleats / to fall and grace curves / when we walk / the gap
between our blouses and our skirts / is bigger than the space
between the ground and our falls / but not greater / than the
rift between our histories and us / 1.4 of us won't remember /
to pin the pallu / before we count the pleats / we will fold the
threaded sari in on itself / and buy sari-inspired jackets / with
labels that cost us more than a flight ticket back / "home" /
I buy bangles from Amazon / because I'm too ashamed / to
walk into a high street shop and ask the uncle for chudiyan /
and pronounce it wrong / my wrists may have been made / for
the constant clanging of glass / against glass / but smashing
the patriarchy / makes me bleed / I bleed vermilion: sindoor /
recognise it not from my relatives / but from daily dramas on
Zee TV and Sony / as the pseudo-shock from the cliffhanger
ending / of that last episode / hits / my sari threatens to undo
itself / expose my pale skin.

1.5 generation immigrant / I am not wholly / second
generation / assimilated / somewhat accepted into a /
community / I am / 'too young when you came here to be first
gen' / but / 'still foreign enough to have a "home" you should
go back to' / I'm not enough / point 5 of me is in another
country / – constantly / point 5 of me is struggling to / turn my
tongue in ways I used to / point 5 of me cries / at the thought
of my children / not being able to hold private / conversations
in public / point 5 of me orders lemon and herb instead of
extra hot / point 5 of me cannot hold a dupatta straight / point
5 of me forgets if this song was an original or a remix / point
5 of me will never remember what channel *Kyunki Saas Bhi
Kabhi Bahu Thi* came on / point 5 of me / point 5 of me / point
5 of me / point 5 of me / turns to the whole of me
and questions her identity / 1.5 of me sits on the borders and
laughs back / one foot in each country / weight distributed so
not to weigh anyone down / I take your spices / and mother
tongue / and sequins and / raags and raise you as a / proud
immigrant.

ii. [insert love cliché here]

smoked kiss

because it's
what you do
when a girl is crying.

when she is baring her soul
telling you how much
she can't live without you
there is nothing else you can do

but call her beautiful
        and press
your lips against hers.
I bit her lip.

told her
her lips tasted of heaven   *(we both cringed)*
I told her I wanted to
taste more apple from the lollipop

she was sucking on earlier.
she informed me that
it wasn't apple
but lime.

she was laughing
when I kissed her again –
this time I could taste her laughter
and it definitely didn't taste of forbidden.

she opened a pack of Marlboro Lights,
        took one to her lips.
I imagined the smoke writhing
on her tongue,

flavouring her mouth.
I took the cigarette from her lips,
snatched the lighter out of her hands,
chick needs to learn to share.

nagina

In the land of the blind, the one-eyed man is king.

Proverb

in towns where
the one-eyed sheikh is king,
brown sugar is dissolved into
gold milk and forced
into the mouths of the
couples newly tied.

           the nagina
waits for the men to throw
their Mashallahs before
silently creeping in and
causing the sheikh to
lose his eye.
they say it is then that
the bed wears her,
her lovers, at one with the curves
of the horizon,
seek shame from their rooms,
spinning gold and lies.
the queens take over
from the sheikh.

for even in a blind kingdom
the snakes still see.

dy: hard to get

the night I saw
her, she was mine.
eyeliner, earthen crow
kisses, lipstick stains
isolated on
         her neck.
she'd look rare,
dishevelled when I was
done, creases from
the sheets down her
         left cheek.
that.
         and a little death.

giving her a green gown

ask her how many times she
rode the wave. answer: not so often.
she finds it rather boring to

lie flat waiting for it to wash over.
others whoop or grunt with effort
but she remains still

with a furrowed brow
riding the high
as high as it goes.

but just like many others
she likes to smoke after.
not so healthy anymore.

wetsuits on the ground, a mixture of
sweat and other juices
all over her body.

naked arms reaching for her pack,
moist neck tilted,
asking for a light.

she cups hands around the end as
though the small burning embers will
provide her with enough

heat to warm her clammy body.
she flops down,
passes her partner the gown

        and has the last bird.
they continue smoking
until it burns to the filter,

                their lips.

black marigolds

– chaandani,
       chaandani.
– did it rain?
– stay.
– the rain took your shape.
– it didn't rain.
       stay. please.

she told him maybe,
to herself counted eight reasons
                 not to.
and then his ada strolled in.
eight reasons not to
turned to one reason to stay.
ada was classy –
but even the moon has craters.
the type who probably had
a Möbius strip between her legs
       dated the Brazilian instead.
she was
       a worldly woman knowing about
dawn and dusk and
everything that came between.
though ada had a preference for moonlight,
she ignored chaandani, went straight to
give kiran a line.
– light doesn't bend, and you, kiran, are extremely kinky.
she walked round to chaandani,
looked her up and down,
assessing,
       then playfully slapped her with
a lady's glove.
– what about you, chanda? are you bent?
she elongated the name and
let it roll around her mouth.
chandaani returned the gaze.
– I reflect off what's given to me.

lights now turned on,
chandaani played with his ada.
stood gracefully.
– your ada is really something, isn't she, kiran?
        shame she's always looking for a new dawn.
kiran was pissed,
exited left, followed by her,
        bare.
– is that true, ada? are you?
– I guess.
kiran left.
leaving them staring up
into the sky, looking
        for dead birds.

her sleepless head lay

the only witness
had their back turned

while our story
died a little. together
we were like

wax melting in
May sun, dripping
                        to one side,

pooling in the centre.
the damp daisies had
sheltered, no judgement.

but you turned around
        while the sky fell –
left us fighting for the sun.

iii. straight lines don't meet

mastana

I silently promised him that
in the very likely event of my not
              having an orgasm

I'd fake it.
          not that he cared.

he
          rolled over
and told me about her roop.
made him want to find her a thousand ships.

I cleaned up –
pretended I wasn't in love with him,
let him continue to tell me more about her.
          even though her face is flat,
          her features are flat,
          her curvature is flat,
          her roop,
          Mashallah,
          makes me deewana.
he continued to talk as I moved
to the bathroom.

I couldn't hear what he was saying
anymore. I wasn't going to
          progress any closer,
couldn't stand the smell of rejection.

I decided:
I was going to tell him
          exactly how I felt,
right after I buttoned up
the remains of his
favourite dress shirt.

I'd rehearsed the conversation
a thousand times in my head.
          – we need to talk.
after that, it went arse over tits.
ten minutes of me singing like a crow.
I rolled up a spliff
and left his house wearing
                    a cliché.

kora's kagaz

there are moths
        crusted onto the walls
from where her copy
of *Cannery Row* killed them.

a live one flies amidst the makeshift grave.
the book is too far.
        – it's your lucky day,
it's a Sunday.

she turns her back to the moth
as if giving it the silent treatment
will make it go away.
        it persists and

annoys her, flying into
her line of sight
        again.
it irritates her even more

when he breathes.
she knows he's there,
he knows she knows he's there.
              but still he breathes

so fucking loudly.

the book
suddenly comes into reach.
     she grabs it and
– yeah. that's right. come

        fly at me now.
– who you talking to?
– the dead moth.
– you know it can't reply, right?

        and not just because it's dead
– I know.

that's why I do it.
he turns to face her,

watches her inspecting
the back of the book
as if waiting for the moth to
                    resurrect itself.

she puts the book down and then
a few minutes later inspects it again.
he knows what's coming.
– don't…

he recoils,
            a pathetic attempt to move away.
it's too late,
the remains

now wiped down his arm.
– you're a bitch. you know that, don't you?
– yep.
                she pops the p and gives back a cheeky grin.

            – you love me for it.
it's a statement, not a question,
but he takes everything as a question.
he muzzles his face in her breasts,

                kisses her gently,
then purposefully brushes his arm against hers.
he starts swirling molten sludge in his mug.
how to turn the answer into a poem or a joke –

a double entendre.
she watches as he walks up and away.
she now knows why he spoils
his look with crushed velvet and

                Brylcreem.

love dies on railway tracks

her task for the day was to find love.
                            not be in it.
it certainly wasn't to fall

madly in love with the person
on the end of the cigarette.
all she could think of was his lips,

how his mouth would taste a little savoury
after smoking.
           she was mid-thought,

thinking about his tongue –
all the things she wanted him to do with it –
when it dawned on her.

           no condom.
– protection,
           she whispered.

           this was pillow talk.
his first thought:
           – thought you were on the pill.

what he said was:
– mixed-race babies are cute.
that ended the 'talk'.

she sunk her head deeper into the pillow.
the following morning, he bought a
turtleneck. being told

not to scream has its consequences.
she still walked with him.
           everywhere he went,

together along tracks,

him walking two steps ahead,
her trying to take long

meaningful strides behind him.
          never catching up.
not until he permitted –

stopping and expertly tapping
a nicotine tube out of its box,
          lighting it.

he stopped by a homeless person,
          huddled,
arms doubling as a blanket and a shield,

and he offered him one.
          he accepted.
anything to keep warm.

when she looked at her lover,
waiting for an explanation, he replied,
          – I'm fixing the world's overpopulation crisis.

Matthew 11:06

violet. her lipstick clung
to his face like an ardent
lover. she would
take long walks to the supermarket and wish upon chemtrailing
conspiracy planes.

took photos of lampposts
            in the dark.
favoured finding work above
finding love.
she watched as his

shape lingered in the rain.
– Matthew, you'll catch a cold. come inside.
            – I'm washing your lip stains off.
– it's eleven o'clock at night.
            – no, it's not.

– 11.06, actually.
            – blessed is anyone who does
            not stumble
            on account of me.
– are you high or something?

            – no. but you understand,
            don't you?
she didn't even try.
the sex was good and
            he was there.

ninety-day wonders

zero
the pain in her uterus was
scraping. she could feel

       shearing, tearing,
vibrations through the walls.

hell, she could hear scrapping sounds.
in a few swift well-rehearsed moves,

she fell into the bathroom,
managing to hold her head

       above the toilet
in time for her stomach to vomit out

          nothing else.

eating had become impossible.
sickness hadn't.

she wiped her mouth,
moving the sweat and

other fluids to her sleeve.
the warm morning upon her,

floor tiles cooling her neck,
       creasing thighs.

within seconds
sitting up again,

ready for the second wave.
this time the pain went on, up

       and through.

her muscles spasmed,
cried out for the Lord to have mercy,

give strength.
drinking the water quick,

trying to keep urges to puke at bay,
she wondered if pain could be distracted.

as if on cue
                        her uterus turned.

no time to wipe the toilet seat,
she sat,

evacuated her bowels
and everything else that came.

the mourning rose through the window.
she felt better now.
                        at peace.

minus one
he had told her that
the words *sunset* and
sunrise were false.

but it was only now,
watching the world become
the colour of sweet condiments,

that she realised
the man might not have just
been trying to get into her pants.

clouds pregnant and bursting, braised.
if she cried alone and
no one heard,

would she make a sound?
she smiled inaccurately.
swallowing the last bite

       of her handout.
she stared up
       to see the wishes blown

       on dandelion clocks
       floating down
       the sky.

minus two
he strongly suggested
             she drink.
impolite not to.
better the taste of bitter

       than the taste of blood.
she (in uncharted territory)
would have to do as told.
he bit through her name the first time.

the second time it hurt.
stroking markings on her arms,
she calmed herself,
became an easy surrender.

she promised God,
         save me and
     I'll save myself from sin,
but God wouldn't lose anything either way.

in between the spots of red on the fluoro light,
broken glass and the dented pan
he sat exhausted.
he was angry that

he was angry.
anger didn't dissipate like
her shrinking reflection in the
broken bulbs did.

they sat in silence.

minus three
decisions had been made.
he wanted to do something
romantic. a sweet gesture
like they show in the movies. where
       legs become jelly,

       eyes shout *fuck me.*
he went to find candles,
left her sitting at the table
sipping Shloer.
Mother had always said

moonlight hid all imperfections.
candlelight led to dessert
in the bedroom.
he wanted dessert.
       she didn't.

he was adamant,
crossing seven seas.
he rooted through his man-drawer.
picked up the closest thing.
           the flashlight would do.

minus four
he.
a similar shade of not-white.
barged into you by accident.
skinny latte spilling over your new blackbird coat.
he apologised,

> stuck out his hand,
> offered to buy you a drink.

you don't.

couldn't do your name justice
> but over dinner
explained your sexuality to you.
made you wonder
what it would feel like,
> his fingers,
> your nipples,
> to have his stubble graze
> your thighs,
expounding upon the wonders
in his world.

you came out too young,
> he said,
and you entertained the idea to
stop him talking.

something about the way
> his lips moved.

later, you wondered if he was right.

daisy chains aren't just for children

he was to propose to her every
day with a daisy ring; every day

because they would wilt;
rings are promises; every day he'd

leave the estate to go
out and pluck one

from the park across
the road and make a ring

for her; diamonds are
bloody, daisies are cute,

she told him,
so there he was,

trying to find daisies in
December; he

started refrigerating them, tried
planting them in his house, watering

religiously; when that didn't work he
killed their friends, and gave them to her tied up,

used them to show that unlike
the daisies, his love for her

was undying.

the other side of the morning

as onions lead to other dimensions her heart led to darker things. razors don't shine in the sun or the lightbulb like you think. she hadn't walked home in over a year. she ran. at 4am. she would run from home and then run to it. again and again until the streetlights flicked off and her blonde highlights stopped uplighting in the moonlight. light. he walked into the bar and ordered water. he wasn't a customer. couldn't be. carried a chip in his pocket and one on his shoulder. after downing his last glass leaving ice cubes clinking in the bottom he left.

4.30am.

a walk down memory lane. she turned left. running from her dreams, to her white dress? who knew. for him, she was running. so he followed. he ran behind chasing her. what came over him? he hoped she would. her blonde highlights turned grey and they still ran. him behind her.

iv. does each line have
two sides?

she has father issues

her father didn't abandon her.
she abandoned
                        him.

Dolly

he leaned towards his daughter
and two flowers bumped into each other
                              in the wind.

she'd reached the age
where she began to see that
having dark hair and fair skin meant

Snow White would have razor burn.
she just didn't have anyone
to explain an alternative.

her mother,
            fair-skinned,
            light-haired,
            was well read,

but it didn't stop her daughter
from growing up with scribbled doll faces.
Dolly gave them Britney haircuts and

when she couldn't find scissors
would take the hair out in chunks.
once the dolls became too mangled,

she started on herself.
            they were made in her image, after all.
her father was aloof.

he loved her mother
            like he did her.
when he did come around

he made her watch.
his daughter was made in
            her image, after all.

summer is for falling in love with

he needs you the reader to imagine them, for if you don't exist, they don't.

i

he peels the skin and waits
for the air to hit them.
            hardening. curled
up, they shrink, leaving
him with petals that
never belonged to flowers.
he looks to you and you
            don't question it.
the colour darkens and in
an instant he
            realises,
no matter what the choice,
            oranges only blossom in
May.

ii

Perse-phony
was her favourite character.
in all the myths he read to her,
hers was the only one that felt
true. she would sit and thread
dried flowers to wear
            round his neck
until each piece
broke with staleness,
leaving sharp brown
edges to pierce her
            underfoot.

he called what they sat in
not silence, but *mokita* –
      a truth they both knew
but agreed not to talk about.
                 she called it lies.

iii
he watches her, tells her
he loves her. somehow
acknowledges that
      it is wrong. long hair
sweeping her face tempts him
to touch her, feel her
soft smooth skin
      upon his.
what he loved
      about her face?
it had never borne the marks of pain, nor
guilt, nor fear.
she wore the same perfume
as her mother – he thought it
      romantic. and then she
turns. and just like that,
      he remembers.
      she is his
      child.

father's day

a
she gets up
in the middle of the night
to relive herself. in the light
of the lamppost outside
she looks white, her colour
is outshined and her hair, it
darkens for a moment,
            making me feel a dwarf.
she could glide through life
on the desires of others
                        and she does.

yet there are times
I'd like the opportunity to say yes,
instead of always being
            the one to ask.
the way she looks at me, it's
wrong to look at someone like that
            when you don't love them.

b
there's something to be said
about men
who aren't the heroes
of their own dreams, nor
are they the ones being saved.
he just stood there, on
            the sidelines, kicking dead
balls around. he muttered a tune
about praying mantis,
didn't care much for beads and
            crossed her.

you forced yourself,
but know that Moses, he

                parted the sea with
                                his tongue.

c
when the wind blew
he shared a smile with a
stranger because looking at her
                was too hard.
he grazed her ankles,
kept her high in the grass.
her skin birthing
icicles where his fingers
                        once were. she had
preferred the adventure section
of the bookshops.
escapism and action.

now the books wrote themselves.
bound themselves and
                sold themselves.
the card lay
on the mantelpiece
                        unread.
from then on he avoided Sundays.

100 years

the first
beads of water drip
long stems of grass.
the sun rises, warming
fields after a cold night's work.
little daisies, small, white,
yellow-middled,
some with pink tips, sit in
          small clusters: little women
gossiping about the new family
on the block. slowly
they open, receive rays of light.

the second
one could say that she was
dumped, if it weren't for the
          way she was lying.
one would easily be
mistaken into thinking
that the young girl was indeed
          taking a nap. her eyes
closed, peaceful
on her now-pale face,
          a modern sleeping beauty.
no kiss would wake her.

the third
dead daughters hurt
more than dead fathers.
but as fathers wish their daughters undead,
their daughters don't.
this father tried to wake her.

v. izzat/sharam

the girls who lived

daughters who live past their first day
are wrapped in izzat and shame
and still they wonder why
the girls grow up wearing
guilt and marrying men who
break glass tables,
        not glass ceilings.

maroon wrapped in gold

they make her wear red
on her wedding day
so that when she bleeds
it doesn't show.
gold adorns her wrists
so that when she cooks
she's reminded of the
        burning.
but the red dress
protects her lack of
        virginity
and the gold, she
counts that and
keeps it close to her heart,
        an escape route.

Ganga water wanted

they buried him. Kranti,
a single jasmine flower in her hair,
returned to a place of reincarnation
wearing only white –
      a colour reserved for innocence and death.
there would be no fire
following this procession.
      nothing to mark
the transition from
one life into the next.
instead
      she would wait
      for the dirt to
      fill his last gasp
      before throwing the
      remainder of the flowers
               on top.

sindoor

she knew
when he asked her
that this would not be easy.
he had screamed it
at the top of his lungs
and the words felt unfamiliar to him.
she outright rejected him.
but once the mangalsutra
was round her neck
the heavy weight felt comforting.
it pulled her down to her knees,
leaving her a fish and
him a dominion.
that was how they found her.
scratched temples and blood in her parting.
the sign
        of a committed woman.

republic

next to each cemetery
        is a B&B.
greeting the dead is tiring
and when love runs out, funerals
        double up as nets.
she had started as most people
end: with a library, filled with books
never to be taken off the shelves but
        that she could quote from.

her eulogy too –
people she didn't know
that could quote her.
orange, white and green
draped her, though nationalism
was never her strong suit. over
        saris she wore Nehru
jackets and underneath them
tied black thread to her
neck, hoping, one day, the
prayers would cancel curses
and her honour
        would be saved.

it is difficult to say with her body
closed between wood
        if she were saved
        would her honour be.
the B&B installed a plaque in her memory.

.

she was on her,
       period.
purple nails scratching skin to ease pain.
she slept on the side, large
stomach acting as a carrier for
anxiety. soft food to fill
holes she would never
feel. and he,
he waited and waited.

                never
saw a single tear from
her eye. because he knew
she never liked baking cakes.
instead he watched the rum
run. kept his smiles to
himself and showed a face
worth mourning for.
nails marred her skin again. every
time blood fell, so did
       her skin bleed.

triad

1

they say when you die
your whole life flashes
before you. for her,
as she lay in a pool
of her own piss,
she flashed.
            every sin, every
thing she had ever done
wrong played before her
on fast-forward. in the few
seconds it took from
feeling warm liquid
pool at her legs to light
brown skin turning rosy
red she had relived
65% of her life.

3

to get her interested
in him, he had told her
that harbour porpoises
have the fastest copulation speed
known to mankind. she had
no idea why
this attracted her to him,
            but it did. now she was
trying to contain her snorting
while he slept snoring
loudly by her side. the
            half-life of love
was over before they'd
even begun taking it. now
the lit candle looked more
appealing than his body did.

he slept on while the curtains
melted him to the ground.

2
some ants bite and magnifying
glasses exist for a reason.

lesborrist

it was a dark and stormy
day in September.
clichéd, she knew, on the
very anniversary of the solitary
event that had changed her life.
Muslim men demonised
but the women get
the brunt of it. dressed in protective
black clothing that did nothing
to hide the Muslim inside
it, she tried to rectify
the problems created.
but the fear of Muslims wasn't
what bothered her at this
moment in time.
no, that
just meant she would always have a
spare seat next to her
on the bus, for her bag.
it was the patronising
stare, the pitying whispers
that followed her round
that she hated. they under-
   estimated her.
she wasn't
submissive.
she wasn't being
oppressed.
so on that day in
September, she made use
of her engineering degree and
made her way down to the
old smoke. cigar in hand
and niqaab pinned to the
side, she watched her handiwork
from a quaint little hipster café.
   art terrorism, the news called
it. she called it desire.

vi. thirty-six times she fell

thirty-six times she fell

answers, based on the 1997 study
showing that
answering thirty-six specific questions
leads to intimacy
and can make any two people
fall in love.[1]

one
even the best
dinner guests come
only once. she,
time and time again.

two
fame could never compare
to the way that trees
attract thunderstorms and
lightning.

three
there are too many variables in a phone call. she
wasn't one
of them.

four
perfect days depend on the stuttering sun,
its last words, and her still-wet hair
shakes silver into the night

---

1   Aron, A, Melinat, E, Aron, EN, Vallone, RD, and Bator, RJ. (1997).
    The experimental generation of interpersonal closeness: A
    procedure and some preliminary findings. Personality and Social
    Psychology Bulletin, 23(4), 363–377. Sometimes called 'The 36
    Questions That Lead to Love'.

five
he last sang to himself when the world checked out
and the perpendicular vanished into
       black holes.
he sang deep vowels of
wreckage and chaos.
she saw the untruth
and how hunger kissed his lips.

six
at thirty he had kept
his mind and
her body together.
they froze, locking
broken windows with
door keys.

seven
she had no idea when she would die.
but she knew it would be with her.

eight
three things they
had in common: the
taste for metal,
five times a day
         and the sea.

nine
she is grateful for the way artists
make fake sunflowers
weep. she keeps a dozen in
ceramic so they collect
dust from everyone

ten
she didn't want to change
anything about the way
she was raised, just that
chocolate chips be
used in place of
                            raisins.
he, however, was lactose intolerant.

eleven
his life in detail
didn't excite her; she
favoured product
over process. he
liked knowing how to tell
          a good story.

twelve
if one could
have the ability to never
love at all, I'm not
sure she would choose
that. just as she wouldn't
choose to leave
used condoms
lying on the kitchen
                        floor.

thirteen
things she wanted
          to know:
does she?

fourteen
she dreams of
watching the world
through his hair, pulling it
and guiding his face to
          pleasure.

fifteen
her greatest accomplishment to date no one.

sixteen
she values most in
friendship what
she values in his
love, the way he
names broken
          chairs and empty
glasses.

seventeen
treasured memory no.
          27: your hands
on my thigh as the grass
gives refuge to the
          ants that crawl up
                    my leg.

eighteen
as blue
moons and true love,
terrible memories don't
exist.

nineteen
if in one year she would
die, paper cups
would be handed out at
her funeral. he would light
them all and notice
        only his ash amongst the embers.

twenty
like rotten teeth, friends
can't be
saved by flossing

twenty-one
affection to me is a daisy chain
left intact on a broken pave-
        ment. the sky
breaking surfaces to fall
on her.

twenty-two
five things they share: ink smudges on bent
postcards, the way
rain soaks into their
kurtas, a bed, time
anxiety.

twenty-three
her childhood was Hallmark
cards and refrozen ice cream.
she would guess how old
the town was and always
        come up short.
flowers had made up for missing
years and broken
        birthday candles.

twenty-four
his relationship with his mother
was why she left. why pink-eyed rabbits
are chained to the front
gate, she will never
understand. instead, she'd count
the space between lamp
posts and let snow
grace her skin.

twenty-five
we can both in this room
feel the buzzing of a bee
in our ears. we smell the rain
before it comes and I
nudge you to bring the washing
                                in. you don't.
the wet clothes sit on
us and the bee still –

twenty-six
she wishes she could
share: the way your spine
            twists when you
lie. instead she shares the name
of the tree you hung your
            self from.

twenty-seven
if we were to close
all distance between our sun and
our moon our
earth would lose out. so
we keep our gap   lest
we kill our love before it begins.

twenty-eight
what I like about you: the
way your laugh turns
every head and your feet
        stay uncovered.

twenty-nine
falling up the stairs and falling
in are very similar. both
leave you feeling embarrassed

you missed a step.

thirty
tears that
fall on prayer mats carry truth –
he last cried holding her body, wrapped
her in white muslin and
        salah.

thirty-one
waves don't crash into each other / they absorb / joining to
penetrate rocks or pebbles – him / he sat / still / alive / cold
stiffening him / oceans spoke of climaxes and sexual clichés /
even if he was present / he couldn't have heard her / footsteps /
crunching stones with each stride / whatchya doing? / he heard
that / watching the waves / what they telling you? / the sun's
about to rise / the waves told you that? / nah, Google / waves
didn't tell me shit.

thirty-two
the only thing too serious
to be joked about is how
it would be a sin to not
        kiss you. even with alcohol

on your tongue – I am willing to
take that sin if it means I
            don't commit the first one.

thirty-three
regret is an overused
term and love a mis-
            used one. she
used it to mean jumping
in front of flying bullets and
            he used it to fuck her.

thirty-four
not everyone
has a melting point. porcelain
dolls keep their shape, but crack.
she could endure losing the world
before burning the house down.

thirty-five
when asked whose
death she'd find the most
disturbing she replied yours.
your leaving would split one minute
into sixty seconds and still
            one would
remain missing.

thirty-six
she opened the curtains and let
in the fall. nothing felt quite
as good as stuck-on sweat.
salt could be
mined. and after tasting,
            Kalia would die.
but what will happen to you?

vii. pleas(ur)e

basic

asalamwulaykum, filastin
hurratan, habibi.
he had learned three phrases
from Google for her
in Arabic. she listened and
smiled. her mother had raised her right.
he was looking for love in Palestine.
                              she wasn't.

when people who have not had
the chance to become elders
became ancestors, she'd cry.
momentarily he soothed
her. he spoke to her of
the land. dis land, dis place.
displacement. that place
was never yours. the land
was never yours. but maybe,
maybe the sky will always
          remain ours. he wrapped
the keffiyah he'd ordered
from some online dealer
round his throat. keeping
green, black, red and white
spotted around framing his face.
he saw as she stared at the red,
wondered if she liked the sun.
did she stare at it until the
black spots blurred the
certainty of her future? or
did she loathe it,
hoping it wouldn't return
          the next day?

what it didn't shine upon
          she could pretend never happened.

dates

her mother bought her blue bras as a reminder. but to her, a woman's voice was her nakedness. her mother watched on as she burned them one by one and threw stones at the mirror instead.

he rang her, Gauri

I do not come with
timeless truths when I say
that he has never

known the touch of a lover.
you can tell.
the way he squeezes

fruit to check their ripeness.
his fingers have not yet
experienced tenderness,

nor has his body. kept
away, sheltered from
not just the desire of

others, but his own too.
he was taught not to
love, but to fuck. as

boys are taught to
grab and pull and
girls are taught to take it.

he reads Fanon, but empty
tubes of Fair & Lovely
sit in his drawers.

he may have been woke.
but he, digging into his
own skin to find meaning,

still sleepwalks into white women.

palm fruit

behind closed doors,
broken hinges, lie
unhinged mental states.
kadak chai with burnt milk

                  greets him.
she has to tell him that
coconuts aren't juiced and
still he doesn't believe her.

she is familiar with the shape
of his palms, while he
only talks of their love in palm
trees and stoning mangoes.

the white man is dying

dead blackbirds plagued her dreams.
she wished
           they did him
instead.

jinn

they both had the gin in
them, yet she loved in *english:*
a distant, vanilla sort of love.
instead of love being this
freeing and risky emotion
it became almost stifling.
she got up and stared out the window,
counting the petals on a half-closed daisy.
it held more for her than the bed did.

fighting the patriarchy

there is nothing they can do
that she has not already
done to herself.
she stares at herself,
a mirror.
a version
stares back.
white lines chop her body.
she cocks her head to
the right,
to the left,
as if trying to find something.
she leans in close, kisses
her own mouth – full
with tongue.
the burn delays.
liquid splashes on her face.
she winces, but not
from the pain.
that comes later.
there is no turning back now.

potaachi bhas vs maaim bhas

my mother tongue
fought the language
of my stomach.
         the stomach won.

hungry eyes meet
with the colonised –
there is only one way
         this can go.

the stomach ate the
language of my mother.
her love for her desh
would be overpowered by

her love to belong.
names changed,
hair dyed and along
with it

         my tongue.

viii. for my mother, who sometimes worries that no one will marry me

mother tongue

my mother's mother tongue is Konkani
but she uses my father's language at home.
we have to
because having multilingual arguments in the house
would confuse MI5 and,
well, we're just too kind for that.

so instead we speak Urdu:
            a language of love,
            the language of poets,
but all my mother ever hears are
the butchered slang words
young boys sling at each other
on the bus.

my mother's mother tongue is Konkani but outside
the house she uses *English* –
            God forbid anyone think she's a freshie.

she's learnt to not roll
her Rs and use *only*
only sparingly, but still
she gets asked:·
            where is your accent from?
hears cheap imitations of a voice
she's tried so hard to shake
on TV and film
and it reminds her of what she sounds like
            to the rest of them.

my mother's mother tongue is Konkani
but sometimes she speaks Hindi,
like when we're out shopping
talking about the guy who just queue-jumped in front of us.

she smiles when she speaks it.
            head up. proud.

brings her closer to home.
but then, she has to revert back
to the language of the colonisers
to finish the tale and
        suddenly her head lowers.

my mother's mother tongue is Konkani
but the only time she ever speaks it
is over the phone to
her mother on
        Sunday mornings.

I watch her struggle sometimes
as she tries to remember the word for
        fruit but instead
replaces it with *English* or Urdu. she blames it
on her growing age.
        I know she's forgotten.

mujhe mai che bas Konkani;
        so should mine be.

I dread the day my grandmother passes, for
I'm afraid my mother will lose her tongue.
she won't speak with proudness or
chat back with slickness.
        and my mother's tongue
        will feel foreign in her mouth.

glossary

FAO: colonised tongues

asalamwulaykum: commonly shortened to salaam or butchered by young South Asians as slaaalaykum.

Ambedkar: people often read Arundhati Roy's introduction to his text Annihilation of Caste. people are wrong.

awrah: a superpower that women have to be able to seduce men with their soft and alluring voices.

chai: venti, with almond milk and extra chai, is my order from Starbucks.

coconut: a fruit to be thrown at traitors.

desi/deshi: from the homeland. can refer to people or food items like ghee.

English: a language forced onto colonised beings while Britain was trying to earn its 'great' title.

freshie: an endearing term used to describe a person (or group of people) who has recently arrived in the UK, often by rocking boats.

habibi: the word that *that* beautiful Arab man once called you.

halal: anything that's less than 1% haram.

haldi: the Hindi word for the spice that white hipsters have only just discovered. often found in the form of stains on the edge of plastic containers that once carried curries or turmeric lattes.

haram: anything that's less than 99% halal.

hijab: more than just a piece of cloth that has holes in from where the pins have pulled.

home: the place you think of when you're somewhere else.

immigrant: only valid if they are good. read Nikesh Shukla's The Good Immigrant (Unbound, 2016).

kadak chai: my actual preferred tea order, available at 'my mum's house'.

Kiran: a name for fe/male Indians that Shah Rukh Khan stutters on.

Mashallah: Arabic word meaning *thankful to God*.

mangalsutra: a more hygienic version of a wedding ring.

mango: an attempt from the diaspora to connect to a homeland that they don't recognise.

mother: heaven lies at her feet. lie to her at all times.

mushaira: a poetry open-mic night made up mainly of men who write love and lust poems about being intoxicated by God.

sari: a piece of cloth around nine yards long, held together with safety pins and society's expectations of women.

terrorist: someone who induces terror into the hearts of a group of people. can only be Muslim or Irish; everyone else is a freedom fighter.